The
Management Ideas
of
Nick Saban

A Leadership Case Study of the Alabama Crimson Tide Football Head Coach

Leadership Case Studies

Table of Contents

Introduction

Background Information about Nick Saban

Part One: Mindset - How To Think About Success

Part Two: Preparation - Creating A Culture of Excellence

Part Three: Performance - Executing At A High-Level

Conclusion

Nick Saban's Keys To Success

Nick Saban Quotes

Additional Case Studies

About Leadership Case Studies

Introduction

The role of a head coach at a top ranked college football program is very similar to that of a modern day CEO. Here are just some of the roles that a successful, college football coach must do in order to be competitive.

- Coach and develop 85 scholarship student athletes. This includes preparing them for games, making sure they are meeting their academic requirements, helping them navigate through any personal problems, and preparing them for future employment if they are good enough to play in the NFL.
- Manage his own coaching staff, graduate assistance, and support staff and get them to buy in to the same vision, culture, and standards.
- The college coaching industry is very fluid, with a high turnover rate each year. After each season, assistant coaches frequently move on to run their own programs or find other opportunities. Thus, the head coach must constantly find new staff and get them to buy into their culture each year.
- Every year there is a large turnover as his players either graduate or leave school early to enter the NFL. Thus, the college football head coach must be constantly recruiting and selling his program to high school students.
- The head coach must deal with the media and be the public face of a multimillion dollar program.
- He must appear at public events with financial supporters, charity events, and other functions with the surrounding community.
- He must manage relations with the Athletic Director and University President.

University of Alabama football head coach Nick Saban has managed and led his program to incredible success. He has won 4 national champions, winning 3 championships in a span of 4 years. He has been named Associated Press Coach of the Year twice during his career. He increased the revenue of the athletic department on a yearly basis and raised the profile of the university across the nation. By any metric, Saban has performed like a successful CEO by achieving the goals set out before him.

In this brief Leadership Case study, we analyze and learn the strategies, management ideas, and performance tips of Nick Saban that has made the University of Alabama football program one of the best managed organization in the country.

The lessons learned from this case study can be applied to any team, business, or personal goals that you wish to achieve. You do not have to be a fan of the Alabama Crimson Tide to learn the skills that made NIck Saban successful. Rather, this book takes a business approach and solely focuses on the traits, mindset, and techniques that Nick Saban uses run a high-performance organization.

In fact, you do not even have to be a football fan to learn something from Saban. If you manage people or if you are looking to improve your performance and compete at a higher level, then you will be able to learn the tips from one of the most successful coaches in football.

The case study is broken up in 3 parts to analyze how Saban won 4 national championships throughout his career and constantly competes at an elite level each year.

Part One focuses on the MINDSET of Nick Saban, and the type of mindset he creates within his program. How does NIck Saban set the goals and vision for his program? How important does Saban place on having a positive attitude? We examine examples and speeches where Saban shares his thoughts about creating a successful mindset.

Part Two highlights the PREPARATION that Nick Saban undertakes in order to achieve high-performance. This section focuses on the culture of the Alabama football program. How do you set priorities for your organization? How do you create a culture where everyone has bought in to the same goals and standards?. What does Nick Saban think about time management and how we spend our time on a day-to-day basis? Examples are presented to show how the winning culture was created at Alabama.

Part Three covers the results of the mindset and preparation and shows how it impacts PERFORMANCE. How does the Crimson Tide constantly compete for national championships? How do they handle the pressure of playing under the bright lights? How does the team and players respond to failures and disappointment? Interviews and statements by Nick Saban is highlighted to show how he gets his players to perform at the highest level.

The case study concludes with selected quotes from Nick Saban.

All information in this case study has been collected from public sources. In addition to the footnotes listed in this book, links to the articles, videos and documents are available at our website leadershipcasestudies.com.

Background Information about Nick Saban

Date of Birth: October 31, 1951 in Fairmont, West Virginia

College Education: Graduated from Kent State University in 1973

Head Coaching Experience:
Michigan State University (1995-1999)
Louisiana State University (2000-2004)
Miami Dolphins (2005-2006)
University of Alabama (2007-Present)

Also served as Defensive Coordinator for the Cleveland Browns in 1991-1994 under Bill Belichick.

National Championships:

Louisiana State University (2003)

University of Alabama (2009, 2011, 2012)

5 times Southeastern Conference (SEC) Champion.

Associated Press Coach of the Year: 2003, 2008

Part One: Mindset - How To Think About Success

Vision, Process, and the Discipline to Overcome Circumstances

During his keynote address at a football awards banquet in January 2015, Nick Saban mentioned that many people ask him for advice on how to be successful. Is it having a good game plan? Is it having special offensive and defensive systems? Is it simply outworking the competition?

It's none of these things, said Saban. The most important factor that contributes to success **"is mindset. It's how you think. It's the vision you have for what you want to accomplish."**

According to Saban, the most fundamental aspect of your mindset is to have a vision of what you want to accomplish. This vision is what you strive for on a daily basis, and what sustains you through difficult challenges. The vision has to be the reason why you get up in the morning and put in the hard work.

"We have two sets of eye," Saban said in his keynote. "We have the eyes that see everything that happens, and we have the eyes of the soul, which is what is important to us, what we want to accomplish, what we want to do, and what our vision is."

Once you set your vision, you need to set up a process of things that you need to do to accomplish your vision. We will talk more about this in Part Two, but the basic concept is that you have to put in the work to do what you have to do in order to accomplish your goals and reach the vision you have for your life.

The hardest part in being successful, according to Saban, is having the discipline to stick to the process. Most people can create a vision, and they can figure out a process to reach that goal. But most people lack the discipline to execute on a day-to-day basis.

Saban defines discipline as **doing the what you're supposed to do, when you're supposed to do it, the way it's supposed to be done**. In today's society, there are so many distractions that can easily keep someone from sticking to their process and working towards their vision on a daily basis. "I have this thing over here that I know I'm supposed to do. But I don't really want to do. Can you make yourself do it?," Saban always asks his players. "Then I have this little thing over here that I know I'm not supposed to do, but I want to do it. Can you keep yourself from doing it?"

The way Saban explains it, the discipline to stay true to your vision isn't simply avoiding distractions and mindless entertainment. It also means having the focus, determination, and drive to keep working towards your vision regardless of the circumstances. The circumstances that we all face in life can be hard and difficult, but in order to be successful we cannot let those circumstances affect us from achieving our goals.

Saban brought up NFL head coach Chuck Pagano as an example of a man who focused on his vision and didn't let his circumstances affect him. In his first year coaching the Indianapolis Colts in 2012, Pagano was diagnosed with leukemia at the start of the season. Due to his treatment, he was unable to be with the team after his diagnosis.

Midway through the season between his treatment, Pagano was able to be in attendance for a Colts game. Indianapolis beat Denver in that game, and Pagano made an appearance in the locker room after the game to congratulate the players. In a speech that inspired and touched all who watched it, Pagano said that his circumstances of getting cancer is not going to affect his vision.

"I mentioned before the game that you guys were living in vision, and you weren't living in circumstances," said Pagano. "Because you know where they had us in the beginning -- every last one of them. But you refused to live in circumstances, and you decided consciously, as a team and as a family, to live in a vision. And that's why you bring things home like you brought things home today. That's why you're already champions, and well on your way."

Pagano continued, "I've got circumstances -- you guys understand it, and I understand it. It's already beat." As the players applauded his courage, and his breath shallow due to the fatigue from his treatment, Pagano shared how his vision is helping him get past the challenges.

"And my vision that I'm living is to see two more daughters get married, dance at their weddings, and the hoist that Lombardi (Trophy) several times. I'm dancing at two more weddings, and we're hoisting that trophy together, men."[1]

The strength and dignity with which Pagano fought his cancer inspired his team and the surrounding community to adopt the term "Chuck Strong." By the next season, Pagano was on the sidelines coaching the Colts. In the 2014 season, Pagano was able to get the Colts to the AFC Conference Finals. Although they lost that game to the New England Patriots, in just two years since being diagnosed with leukemia Pagano had his team one win away from playing in the Super Bowl.

There will be times in your life when you face situations that you feel may prevent you from achieving your goals. But it is important to just view them as circumstances, and that you can get past them and stay focused on your vision. Striving towards your vision will give you the strength to overcome any challenges and circumstances.

---

[1] Doug Farrar, "Chuck Pagano gives inspiring, amazing postgame speech to victorious Colts Team, Yahoo Sports, Shutdown Corner, November 4, 2012.

Be Prepared for Difficulties

One way to help you overcome challenging times is to simply accept that they are simply a part of life. One of lines that Nick Saban likes to quote from is from a book called *The Road Less Traveled*, by M. Scott Peck. Saban likes to share with people the first line from the book:

"Life is difficult."

Saban likes this quote because it simply tells it how it is. To be a champion, to be the very best that you can be everyday, is hard. It is hard to strive for excellence every day. But that is simply life. Saban wants all of his players and coaching staff to know that there will be challenges and difficulties in the journey ahead. It's not easy playing in the best football conference in America. It's not easy competing for national championships. Saban argues that it's not supposed to be easy. If the vision and task you are attempting to accomplish wasn't difficult, then is it really a worthwhile goal? The reason why we strive for certain things is because it is difficult and hard, and the journey of overcoming them is what makes the achievement so special.

He makes sure that everyone, from the coaching staff to the players, fully understand that the work that they will be putting in is difficult. Once all of the players and staff understand that the road will be tough, then everyone can accept it and move on.

For example, when practicing in the hot southern sun in Alabama, everyone is suffering through the heat. Since everyone already knows that it's hot, and that everyone is uncomfortable, there is no need to complain about the heat. Accept that it is hot, accept that it difficult, and move on to accomplish the task in front of you to the best of your ability.

Too often, we try to avoid the difficulties in our lives. We try to avoid the difficult choices we have to make, or avoid the difficult work that we need to do to improve our lives. Instead of avoiding it, Saban prepares his players in advance that life is difficult in the first place. Rather than setting expectations that life is fun, and that a good life is facing no difficult situations, Saban instead teaches his players that the road to excellence is difficult. That facing adversity and challenges is part of the process, and that you should expect to encounter challenges that test you.

Positive Attitude

By accepting that life is hard, how then does his players meet the challenges? How do they get through training days in the hot sun, overcome tough losses on Saturday nights, and keep focusing on their vision to be the best? In order to be disciplined to stay focused on your vision, Saban tells his players and staff that they all must have a positive attitude. Having a positive attitude, being confident in yourself, and expressing positive energy not only helps you fight through trying circumstances, but it also impacts your teammates, your co-workers, and potential customers as well. The positive mindset allows you and your organization to meet any challenges with determination and effort.

In an example of how seriously Saban takes confidence and selling a positive attitude, look at how Saban talks to participants at his football camp. For the past several years, Nick Saban has been running football camps during the summer for boys between the ages of 8 to 14. During the check in process, he individually greets each player and asks them to introduce themselves. He then uses this small interaction as a lesson to the players about how they view themselves, and its impact on the team.

"Everyone made an impression on me by how they did it," Saban says in his opening remarks to the camp. "**Because every minute of every day you're selling something. You're either selling positive, or you're selling negative**. And when you put your head down and I can't even hear where you're from, you're not selling positive. You're not selling confidence."

Keep in mind that these are boys between the ages of 8 to 14. Nick Saban is easily the most popular and well-respected man in the state of Alabama. Yet, he teaches young boys that they need to be confident in themselves and to present a positive self-image, regardless of the situation. "You don't have to be intimidated by me," Saban tells the camp. "You look me right in the eye, say your name, and let's have a conversation."

Review Questions:

1. What is your vision? What is it that you or your organization is working towards everyday? If negative circumstances arose and life became difficult, will your vision be able to sustain you? Is your vision meaningful enough to you that you will stay committed to it no matter the circumstances?

2. How do you approach difficulties? When you face a challenge, do you give up? Say that the world is against you? Think that the odds are stacked against you? Instead, start to view difficulties and challenges simply as a part of life. Accept that life is hard and that whatever it is that you are trying to accomplish will be difficult. By fully understanding that life is difficult, you won't be surprised or discouraged when you face challenges.

3. In your interactions with other people, what are you selling? Are you selling yourself or your organization in a positive way? Or are you selling a negative image? If you think in a positive manner, and that you can accomplish your tasks, then that positive energy will help you overcome any difficulties you face.

Part Two: Preparation - Creating A Culture of Excellence

How you spend your time plays another key role in determining your success. If you are wasting your time by not being productive, then you will not be able to compete at the highest level.

Time Management

Nick Saban likes to tell his audience to ask themselves how they spend their time. "**Are you spending your time, or are you investing your time?**" When you invest your time, you are working towards your goals. You are putting the work in to make sure that your efforts are being directed towards the process that you set out for yourself.

When you are spending time, according to Saban, you're basically wasting your time. As he told his football camp, "When you're spending time, you're playing Xbox. And I know all of you will say 'I need my relaxation time'. You know what I say to that? And excuse me to all the Mamas that are here, but that's bullshit. You don't need to do that."

This concept is built into the football program at Alabama. When Strength and Conditioning coach Scott Cochran took reporters on a tour of Alabama's $9 million 37,000 square foot weight room, he emphasised the functionality and efficiency of the room setup. Each workout station was designed so that the players would not have to waste time or effort moving between each exercise.

During practice, Saban structures it so that every conditioning drill, every rep, every action taken on the practice field has been thought out and planned accordingly. Other successful head coaches believe that Saban structures his program so efficiently that if Saban does it, then it must be the best way to do something. Super Bowl winning head coach Bill Belichick of the New England Patriots hired Saban as his defensive coordinator back in 1991 and still keeps in contact. In explaining their relationship to Fortune magazine, Belichick stated that he still talks to Saban, and freely takes ideas and plans from him when needed.

"If I ask Nick a question and he says, 'Well, this is how we do it,' then I usually just cut to where he is and take that shortcut and say, 'Okay, we're going to do it this way.'", says Belichick. "I know that he's already gone through all the stages of thinking it through, and I would rather just get to the stage that he's at rather than waste the time figuring that I'm going to end up at the same point anyway." [2]

It's also built in to the way Nick Saban organizes his daily schedule. Saban has the exact same lunch everyday in order to eliminate thinking about what to order and to save time. So everyday, Saban eats a iceberg lettuce salad with cherry tomatoes with sliced turkey and fat-free honey Dijon dressing. However, Saban has also told the media that he eats the same breakfast of a cup of coffee and two "Little Debbie" cookies when he gets at up 6 AM.[3]

All of these actions are planned out ahead of time so that Saban doesn't waste time. At every minute of everyday, he is working towards his goals. According to one media reporter who interviewed Saban in his office, he uses a remote control to open and close his door in order to save the time it takes to walk there.

Typical Daily Schedule of Nick Saban[4]

[2] Brian O'Keefe, "Leadership lessons from Alabama football coach Nick Saban," Fortune, September 7, 2012.

[3] Lars Anderson, "Nick Saban And The Process," Sports on Earth, July 21, 2014.

[4] Lars Anderson, "Nick Saban And The Process," Sports on Earth, July 21, 2014.

- Wakes up at 6 AM.
- Drinks coffee and eats two "Little Debbie" cookies while watching the Weather Channel.
- Mornings at the office is spent on football matters, meetings with staff, etc...
- Lunch of iceberg lettuce salad with cherry tomatoes with sliced turkey and fat-free honey Dijon dressing served in a Styrofoam container.
- During the offseason, Saban plays in a basketball pickup game at noon after lunch.
- Saban then meets with coaches and players to discuss pressing issues.
- Later in the afternoon and leading into the evening, Saban spends his day watching film of an upcoming opponent, or breaking down film of his own practice.
- During the day, Saban finds time to spend on recruiting. He spends either 30 minutes to several hours working on recruitment. Almost everyday involves some aspect of recruiting players.
- On most days, Saban tries to leave his office by 10 PM.

The actions you take on a day-to-day basis determines whether you are successful or not. The choices you make today will impact how you perform tomorrow.

Nick Saban says that the choices we make are determined by our character. In speeches to the public, Saban says that "character is an accumulation of our thoughts, our habits, and our priorities on a daily basis." How we think, and how we chose to spend our time, will determine whether we are able to achieve the vision and goals that we set out for ourselves.

The Process

At Alabama, Saban has created a culture of excellence by focusing on what he calls "The Process." The Process focuses on the effort and discipline that people put into their tasks. "It's about what you control, every minute of every day. You always have to have a winning attitude and discipline in practice, weight training, conditioning, in the classroom, in everything. It's a process."[5]

The culture at Alabama that Saban has created does not place the emphasis on results. It doesn't emphasis championships, or titles, or how many touchdowns they can score. In fact, Saban tells people that there are no signs about "Winning" inside of the football facility on campus.

Instead, the emphasis is on effort, and doing what you are doing at that moment to the best of your ability. Focusing on the end results serves as distractions, and takes your focus away from doing the best job you can in the moment. Whether it be during the game, during practice, or when you are working out, your focus and attention should be solely on taking that specific action and doing it the best way possible.

"It's the journey that's important. You can't worry about end results. It's about what you control, every minute of every day," says Saban.[6]

Here is Nick Saban explaining his process to the media before the 2012 National Championship game against Notre Dame.

"Well, the process is really what you have to do day in and day out to be successful. We try to define the standards that we want everybody to sort of work toward, adhere to, and to do it on a consistent basis. And the things I talked about before, being responsible for your own-self determination, having a positive attitude, having great work ethic, having discipline to be able to execute on a consistent basis, whatever it is you're trying to do, those are the things we try to focus on, and we don't try to focus as much on the outcomes as we do on being all that you can be."

---

[5] Lars Anderson, "Nick Saban and the Process," Sports on Earth, July 21, 2014.

[6] Lars Anderson, "Nick Saban and the Process," Sports on Earth, July 21, 2014.

"Eliminate the clutter and all the things that are going on outside and focus on the things that you can control with how you sort of go about and take care of your business. That's something that's ongoing, and it can never change."

"So it's the process of what it takes to be successful, very simply."[7]

Jena McGregor, a columnist at the Washington Post who writes a column on leadership, writes how Saban's philosophy can be used to apply to any organization or business:

"Focus relentlessly on recruiting the best people. Define exactly what the job is you want them to do. And then, push them to focus relentlessly on doing just that, rather than looking ahead to the win- or the next game."[8]

"Saban teaches his players to stop actually thinking about winning and losing and instead focus on those daily activities that causes success," writes Jason Seik on the Forbes website. "He encourages his players to adopt a definition of success defined not by the results, but rather by effort. Instead of emphasizing scoring touchdowns, he asks players to define themselves with such things as competing each set in the weight room or completing practices with 100% intensity."

Not focusing on "winning" does not mean that Nick Saban does not care about winning championships. His results clearly says otherwise. But Nick Saban and others who follow this mindset understand that the focus of the goals cannot be on the end result. As Seik writes, **"Focusing on the outcome is paradoxical. The more one emphasizes winning, the less he or she is able to concentrate on what actually causes success."** [9]

---

[7] Greg Bishop, "Saban Is Keen to Explain 'Process'," New York Times, The Quad Blog, January 5, 2013.

[8] Jena McGregor, "How Nick Saban leads the Crimson Tide," Washington Post, November 30, 2012.

So rather than making goals about end results, Saban's process encourages people to set effort goals where you strive to be the very best that you can be. Instead of setting of goal of winning a championship, your goal should be to be the very best at each possible moment. If you are practicing, put all of your efforts into each practice rep. If you are working, put all of your efforts and focus into completing each task to the best of your ability. Whatever you chose to do, make it your goal to put you fullest effort into each single task that you need to do.

Clearly Define Expectations

Saban instills in his players and staff that every single task that they do must be done to the highest standards. In numerous interviews and speeches, Nick Saban mentions his childhood growing up in West Virginia. As a child, Saban worked at his father's gas station, where he would help wash and clean each car that came in. His father would check on the cars that 11 year-old Nick had cleaned, and if there was any dirt or streaks, then Nick would have to clean the car again. Not just the area where the dirt was, but to redo the ENTIRE car. This taught Saban that his father expected each car to cleaned correctly, and that mindset on setting clear expectations has followed him to Alabama.

"You really have to define exactly what the expectation is of everybody in your organization is and everybody on your team and what the standard is," Saban stated in his keynote address. "Because if you don't do that, then people don't know exactly what is expected of them.

"But once it is defined, you have to hold everyone accountable to that. Because **mediocre people don't like high achievers, and high achievers don't like mediocre people.** And if you let those

---

[9] Jason Selk, "What Nick Saban Knows About Success," Forbes, September 12, 2012.

things coexist in your organization, you're never going to have any team chemistry."

That attention to a high-standard to excellence and accountability for your actions is something that in enforced every day at Alabama. Every single task, whether it's a game plan, recruiting, or a weightlifting session, is done to the highest standards. Saban refers to it as "Pride in Performance." Take pride in what you do, and strive to do it to the best of your ability.

Be The Best You Can Be

After winning his 4th National Championship, a reporter asked Saban what was his motivation to keep coaching. As Michael Weinreb wrote in Grantland, "Someone asked Saban a simple question: Why? In other words, why keep doing this, and why keep striving, and why not pull a Spurrier and slip off to the golf course on some August afternoon during a two-a-days and delegate to one's coaching staff?"[10]

To answer the question, Saban referred to a speech given by Martin Luther King Jr. In the speech, King encourages his audience to be the best at whatever you are, even if you are a just a street sweeper.

Here is the text of the speech given by Martin Luther King Jr in Cleveland, Ohio in 1967:

"Set out to do a good job and do that job so well that nobody can do it any better.

If it falls your lot to be a streetsweeper, sweep streets like Michelangelo painted pictures.

Sweep streets like Shakespeare wrote poetry.

---

[10] Michael Weinreb, "The Shadow of Nick Saban," Grantland, January 9, 2013.

Sweep streets like Beethoven composed music.

Sweep streets so well that all the hosts of heaven and earth will have to pause and say here lived a great streetsweeper who swept his job well". [11]

---

[11] Martin Luther King Jr: April 26, 1967, Cleveland speech, annotated, Cleveland Plain Dealer, Edited by John Kroll, January 13, 2012.

Review Questions:

1. How are you spending your time? Really be honest with yourself. Are the things that you are doing on a daily basis directed towards improving your performance? Are you focusing on the right goals and priorities?

2. What type of goals are you setting for yourself and your organization? Are they in your control? If your goals are based upon an external results, such as winning a championship or winning an account, then it might be best to change them to something that is firmly in your control. For example, instead of making the goal a championship, the goal should be for each player to develop the stamina to finish each play with their fullest effort. Think about how you can create process goals instead of result-oriented goals.

3. Is everyone on the same page? Does every person associated with your goals clearly understand what the goal is? If you are an individual, does your family, friends, and significant other fully understand the vision you have for yourself and are willing to support you to achieve it? Does your friends understand that you might not be able to hang out on the weekend? Same goes with your organization. Is everyone held to the same high standards? Is everyone held accountable for reaching the high standard?

Part Three: Performance - Executing At A High-Level

Focus On The Moment

Nick Saban knows the exact date where his coaching philosophy was created. It was November 7, 1988. Saban was then the Head Coach of the Michigan State Spartans. His team was 4-4, and was about to face the number 1 ranked Ohio State Buckeyes, who were undefeated at the time and favored to win the National Championship that year.

Entering the game as 28 point underdogs, Saban felt that he needed to change it up in order to compete. Michael Casagrande of Al.com writes that "Nick Sabn took a different path in the preparation for this game. They weren't going to focus on the result (starting to sound familiar?) They were going to look at each play as a separate entity (ringing a bell?)".[12]

Casagrande goes on to quote Saban talking in the 2010 documentary "Gamechanger".

"We were going to focus on the process that would take to play the best football you could play, which was to focus on that particular play like it had a history and a life of its own. Don't look at the scoreboard. Don't look at any other external factors."

Saban says that each moment was important at that particular moment. Once that play was over, whether it was a successful play

---

[12] Michael Casagrande, "Nick Saban's 'process' was born 15 year ago today with a stunning upset at Ohio State," al.com, November 07, 2013.

or not, "you would move on to the next play and have the same focus". By attacking each play, and doing your very best at each moment throughout the game, then "you would be able to live with the results regardless of what the results were."

The results for this game? Michigan State 28, Ohio State 24.

One of the benefits of focusing solely on the play in front of you is that it makes things much easier for the players. As Joe Posnanski writes in NBC Sports, "It was easier. So much easier. Suddenly everything was manageable. He wasn't asking players to go out and win the game; no, that's too big, too overwhelming, too vague a task."[13]

By not worrying about the score, by not worrying about how highly ranked their opponents were, and by focusing only on the play in front of them, Saban's players were able to knock off the No.1 ranked Buckeyes.

Failure Is An Opportunity To Improve

For a perfectionist like Nick Saban, you would think that he would never tolerate a mistake. However, Saban fully understands that failure is a part of life. He understands that people will make a mistake. But what he expects is that his players learn from those mistakes. If a player does something wrong, he expects that the player will accept the correction from the coaches.

He makes it very clear from the very start that when someone from the staff corrects a mistake, that the coach isn't criticizing the player. It's coaching. It's helping the player improve their performance. So building upon the positive attitude that the player should already have, then any mistake and correction is used as an opportunity to grow and improve.

---

[13] Joe Posnanski, "Alabama Coach Nick Saban Unrelenting in Pursuit of Perfection," NBC Sports, November 8, 2013.

Failure is not viewed as a negative thing. Rather, failure is viewed as an opportunity to improve and grow.

Saban likes to refer to a Nike commercial about Michael Jordan that came out in 1997. The commercial shows Jordan walking into the arena before a game. Jordan provides the voiceover for the ad. This is what he says:

"I've missed more than 9,000 shots in my career.

I've lost almost 300 games.

26 times I've been trusted to take the game winning shot, and missed.

I've failed over, and over, and over again in my life.

And that is why I succeed." [14]

This embracement of failure is a key part of Saban's philosophy. Great performers such as Nick Saban and Michael Jordan understand that failures are a part of life. Rather than expressing disgust or anger at failure, great players and coaches view the mistakes as opportunities to improve. They don't give up, they don't stop trying, and they keep working towards their goals.

Improvement and Adjustment

One way to see how Saban improves on his mistakes is by looking at his record of so-called revenge games. These are games where Alabama faces a team that they previous lost to. From the time Saban took over the program in 2007 to 2013, Saban had 7-1 in these types of games. The average margin of victory was 20.9 points. [15]

---

[14] Eric Zorn, "Without Failure, Jordan Would be False Idol," Chicago Tribune, May 19, 1997.

The mindset of Nick Saban, however, is not revenge, but improvement. The goal is to zero in on the mistakes that were made in the loss, make the proper adjustments, and then perform and execute in a better manner in the next game. It's not about finding ways to motivate the players. It is simply finding ways to get better.

Immediately after losing to Ohio State in the national semifinals in January 2015, Alabama's coaching staff reached out to the Ohio State offensive coordinator to find out how the Buckeyes were able to win. According to a transcript by Al.com, Alabama defensive coordinator told a local radio station that they reached out immediately after losing to find out how they can improve.

"I'll tell you the best thing we did - and I give coach Saban a lot of credit - we went directly to [Herman]... We said, 'Hey, we want to meet with you. You know us better than anybody. You spent four weeks getting ready for us. What's our tendencies? What did we do wrong? What do you think? And he was just honest with us. He told us what he thought, and it was very valuable for us."[16]

There is no ego involved. There is no pride, and no bitter feelings after a lose. Saban and his coaching staff took the loss to Ohio State in stride. Instead of feeling sorry for themselves, they immediately took action to try and fix it. They took the loss as an opportunity to improve. They were relentless in their pursuit to get better.

Relentless:

This relentless is something that Nick Saban likes to see in his players. He likes to use the example of Freddy Krueger from Nightmare on Elm Street. Saban tells his audience that no matter

[15] Chris Low, "For Saban, there are no big games," ESPN, September 13, 2013.

[16] Matt Zenitz, "Alabama coaches had 'very valuable' meeting with Ohio State offensive coordinator following Sugar Bowl," AL.com, July 2, 2015.

how many times you think that you killed Freddy Krueger, he keeps coming back and breaking doors.

That's the type of relentless attitude Saban wants to see from his program. At each moment, no matter what happened the play before, or the game before, or the next game, you play your best at that moment.

Having a positive attitude, being direct with people, and being relentless are some of the traits that individuals in sales needs to have. Being relentless in selling yourself or your organization is a key driver of success, and it is what made Saban into one of the best salesman in the country.

A large part of achieving success in college football is recruiting. In order to find the best players, Nick Saban needs to travel around the country and convince 17 year old boys to commit to his program. He needs to enter living rooms and relate to parents and families of all different backgrounds. He pitches these families on the benefits of his program, and how he can help them achieve their goals.

Traveling around the nation and finding talent is an exhausting job, but Saban does it without complaint. Nearly every day is spent on some aspect of recruiting. Saban has told people that he watches every single high school play of the recruit that Alabama is targeting.[17]

"Ask around about what makes Saban perhaps the greatest living-room pitchman in the history of college football and people mention his directness, his willingness to be honest, his quasi-corporate approach," explains Michael Weibreb. "This is Saban's strength: his program, his process, his record, his system. He forwards the idea of Alabama in the say way that, I imagine, a Wall Street recruiter might sell a Harvard Business graduate on Goldman Sachs." [18]

---

[17] Joe Posnanski, "Alabama Coach Nick Saban Unrelenting In Pursuit of Perfection," NBC Sports, November 8, 2013.

[18] Michael Weinreb, "The Game Within the Sugar Game: Nick Saban, Urban Meyer, and the Battle of College Football's Recruiting Kingpins,"

In the bestselling book *The Blind Side*, Michael Lewis briefly discussed how Nick Saban performs in a living room. Saban was doing a house visit where he was attempting to recruit Michael Oher to LSU.

"Saban came into the house in his Armani suit and Gucci dress shoes and made a point of being polite to every single person in the room. Then he looked around, as if soaking in every last details of the Old English and Country French furnishings, and said, "What a lovely home. I just love those window treatments."

"He knew everything from the names of the people who would tutor Michael to the place on campus where Michael would do his laundry. And he addressed his remarks not only to Michael but also to Leigh Anne. Michael didn't have any questions for him but Leigh Anne did; and he answered them beautifully."

The guardian of the recruit, Leigh Anne, "decided that if Nick Saban wasn't the most polished and charming football coach in America, she was ready to marry whoever was."[19]

Since he's always selling excellence, even the way Saban sets up his office is meant to convey that impression. In a profile by GQ magazine, the writer meets Saban in his office at Alabama. "Saban gravely invites me in and motions me toward the seating area where he meets with recruits and their families. On brass easels to my right are three framed photographs of his Alabama championship teams on the White House steps with President Obama. "Want your son to meet the president?" the photos all but declare. "Let him play for me."[20]

Grantland, December 30, 2014.

[19] Michael Lewis, The Blind Side: Evolution of a Game, W.W. Norton & Company, 2007, page 183-184.

[20] Warren St. John, "Nick Saban: Sympathy for the Devil, GQ, published on August 26, 2013.

Emotional Stability

One of the benefits of focusing on the process and not on the outcomes allows Saban and his players to keep their emotions in check. It doesn't matter if they are playing for the national championship or their in-state rivals, the task at hand is the same. Focus on the individual plays and not about unnecessary things.

ESPN wrote an article about how Saban wouldn't get too high or too low when dealing with big games. Through a relentless focus on the process, Saban is able to focus his team to keep an even keel regardless of the magnitude of the game.

Saban's former offensive coordinator and current head coach of the University of Florida Jim McElwain stated that Saban never seemed to worry about the importance of one game, and made sure that the team was never too high or too excited.

Another former coordinator, Will Muschamp, who was previously the head coach at Florida, stated that Saban was able to keep his players focused on the task at hand by using the process. "It's the same approach every week, no matter how big a game, no matter if it's the national championship, the SEC championship, or if it's the state rival. He approaches every game exactly the same. He spends the same time at the office. He has the same type of preparation. He has the same type of intensity."[21]

Focusing on the moment and the process instead of the results has many benefits. It allows you to constantly work to improve and to stay relentless. Since you are no longer focusing on the results, you don't get nervous or worry about making mistakes. Even when you do make a mistake, you view the mistake as an opportunity to learn, and then make the improvements and adjustment to improve. This mindset creates a constant cycle of performance that is always humming at its peak.

---

[21] Chris Low, "For Saban, there are no big games," ESPN, September 13, 2013.

Review Questions:

1. When you are performing, what are you thinking about? When you are working, are you dreaming about the rewards and payoffs? If you are, then your performance may not be at its peak. Instead, try to focus solely on each task and moment in front of you.
2. When you make a mistake or fail, what lessons are you taking from it? Are you viewing the mistakes as an opportunity to learn and improve? Or are you viewing the mistake as proof that you are no good? View your mistakes as learning opportunities and continue to be relentless in improving.
3. How excited do you get while performing? How nervous? Do you feel like you need extra motivation for certain jobs? Again, this might be because you are thinking about the rewards. Try to focus only on the small task in front of you. This will help keep your nerves and emotions from affecting your performance.

Conclusion

"You have to be a champion before you can win a championship," says Saban.

In order to achieve whatever it is that you are trying to accomplish, you have to do the job that it requires. If you want to be champion, you have to do the work that a champion does. If you want to be rich, you have to do the work that a rich person does in order to become wealthy. If you want to get in shape, then you have to do the things that a person in shape does.

This is why Saban focuses the programs goals on the efforts and not the results. By focusing on the work that needs to be done, the results take care of themselves. Don't worry about the end goal, or how hard it may be. Simply focus on the moment right in front of you and do the work that you have to do.

There is no magic solution to becoming a champion. There is no secret to becoming the best.

"Everybody wants to be a success. Not everybody is willing to do what they have to do to achieve it", says Saban. [22]

---

[22] Jason Selk, "What Nick Saban Knows About Success," Forbes, September 12, 2012.

Nick Saban's Keys To Success

1. Have a vision, create a process on how to achieve that vision, and have the discipline to stick to the process.
2. Set goals that you in your control, such as your effort. Don't set goals about results that are not in your control.
3. Focus on the task in front you. Don't let past failures affect you, and don't let future gains distract you. Stay in the moment.
4. Have pride in your performance. Do your best at everything that you do.
5. You are either investing your time wisely, or you are spending your time.
6. To be successful is hard. Expect difficulties and challenges. Simply accept them and move on.
7. Have the discipline to do the right thing when it needs to be and in the right way.
8. Learn from your mistakes. Don't get defensive when someone is trying to help you.
9. You are selling yourself every minute. What are you selling? Are you selling a positive, confident image?
10. To be a champion, you have to work like a champion. Do what champions do.

Nick Saban Quotes

"You are either investing your time, or spending your time."

"Have pride in your performance."

"Discipline means doing the right thing, at the right time, the right way."

"You are either selling positive, or you are selling negative."

"We have two sets of eyes. We have the eyes that see everything that happens, and we have the eyes of the soul, which is what is important to us, what we want to accomplish, what we want to do, and what our vision is."

"You can't worry about end results. It's about what you control, every minute of every day."

"Mediocre people don't like high achievers, and high achievers don't like mediocre people."

"Do you pray to be blessed? Or do you pray to be a blessing?"

"You can't have any great victory in life unless you overcome adversity."

"You cannot be a good leader if you do not care about other people."

"There are two pains in life. There is the pain of discipline, and the pain of disappointment. If you can handle the pain of discipline, then you'll never have to deal with the pain of disappointment."

"Everybody wants to be a success. But not everybody is willing to do what they have to do to achieve it."

Additional Leadership Case Studies

The Motivational Techniques of Urban Meyer

The Turnaround Strategies of Jim Harbaugh

The Strategy Concepts of Bill Belichick

The Leadership Lessons of Gregg Popovich

The Team Building Strategies of Steve Kerr

The Work Ethic of Tom Brady, Peyton Manning, and Aaron Rodgers

About Leadership Case Studies

Leadership Case Studies provides brief reports and analysis on successful individuals. We focus on the habits, strategies, and mindsets of high-performing people in the sports, business, and entertainment industries.

Started in July 2015, Leadership Case Studies released its first case study on University of Alabama Football Coach Nick Saban, winner of 4 national championships.

Website:
http://www.leadershipcasestudies.com

Made in the USA
Coppell, TX
11 December 2021